children's HISTORY of HARROGATE AND KNARESBOROUGH

Written by
Paul Chrystal and
Anne Chrystal

HOMETOWN WORLD

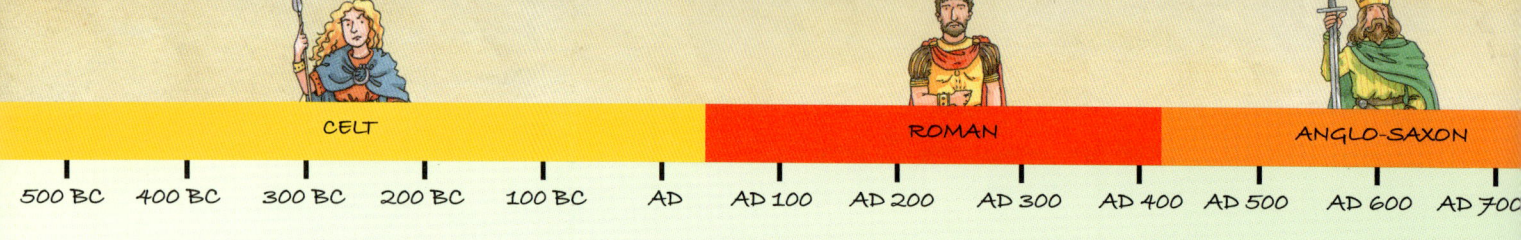

How well do you know your town?

Have you ever wondered what it would have been like living in Harrogate or Knaresborough in Viking times? What about rubbing shoulders with the finest people in the land in the Royal Pump Room? This book will uncover the important and exciting things that happened in your town.

Want to hear the other good bits? You will love this book! Some rather brainy folk have worked on it to make sure it's fun and informative. So what are you waiting for? Peel back the pages and be amazed at what happened in your town.

THE FACTS

Timeline shows which period (dates and people) each spread is talking about

Clear informative text

Hometown facts to amaze you!

THE EVIDENCE

'Spot this!' game with hints on something to find in your town

Intriguing old pictures

Go back in time to read what it was like for children growing up in Harrogate and Knaresborough

Each period in the book ends with a summary explaining how we know about the past

Contents

The Roman Town   4

The Viking Settlement   8

Living in a Castle   10

Mother Shipton   14

Rich and Poor   18

The Royal Pump Room   22

Fairs of the North   26

Harrogate and Knaresborough
Today and Tomorrow   28

Glossary   30
Index   31
Acknowledgements   32

CELT
500 BC

ROMAN
AD 43–410

ANGLO-
SAXON
AD 450–
1066

VIKING
AD 865–
1066

MEDIEVAL
TIMES
1066–
1485

The Roman Town

It has been a long journey and they are tired, but Livia and her parents have finally reached Isurium Brigantum in the north of Britannia. They have come to Isurium for her father's work. Gaius is a lawyer and will work in the basilica (law courts). Isurium is about as far away from Rome as you can get! It's cold, cloudy and wet but they will be comfortable, the underfloor heating will see to that. Livia's villa is one of the largest and most luxurious villas in Isurium. She can't wait to explore her new home!

This will do nicely. Shame about the rain!

Mater, look at the floor, it's beautiful!

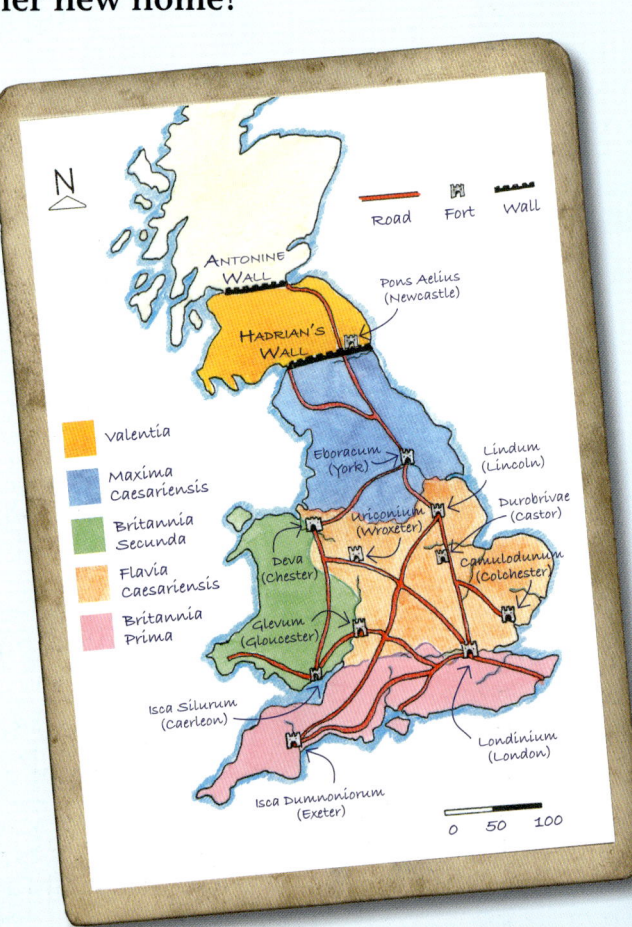

This map shows the main areas, roads and forts in Roman Britain. The Brigantes tribe ruled most of the area coloured blue.

Map labels:
N
Road   Fort   Wall
ANTONINE WALL
Pons Aelius (Newcastle)
HADRIAN'S WALL
Valentia
Maxima Caesariensis
Britannia Secunda
Flavia Caesariensis
Britannia Prima
Eboracum (York)
Lindum (Lincoln)
Uriconium (Wroxeter)
Durobrivae (Castor)
Deva (Chester)
Camulodunum (Colchester)
Glevum (Gloucester)
Isca Silurum (Caerleon)
Londinium (London)
Isca Dumnoniorum (Exeter)
0   50   100

Isurium Brigantum

Isurium Brigantum used to stand where the village of Aldborough is today, 22 km outside of Harrogate. Isurium was once occupied by the Ninth Legion. Their fortress was at Eboracum (the Roman name for York). Isurium was built to defend the area against attack from the Brigantes when they weren't so friendly. The Brigantes were a Celtic tribe who had ruled most of Northern England before the Romans arrived.

Isurium was an important Roman town and became the capital of the Romanized Brigantes. It continued to grow with more luxurious buildings being built, decorated with beautiful mosaics, some of which have survived. It had a forum (that's the market place), a basilica and baths and temples for the Romans to worship their gods.

ABOUT AD 200 ROMANS SETTLE IN ISURIUM AND BUILD DEFENSIVE WALLS...

Daily Life

The items in the museum at Aldborough tell us a lot about how the Romans and Brigantes lived. They were skilled people and introduced new ways of making pottery, glass and metal. Archaeologists have dug up bowls, dishes and cups, all from Roman times. They found amphorae – these are large urns which would have been filled with olive oil, fish sauce (the Romans loved it) and wine.

If you go to the museum you may see other Roman objects, such as metal dress pins, keys and coins. The dice and pins and needles are made from bone. A golden earring, a gold garnet ring and seal rings were also discovered. Seal rings were used by officials in place of a signature on official documents – the most famous one has a picture of a chariot being pulled by a cockerel. Perhaps this belonged to Gaius.

These are some of the urns the Romans left behind.

The Romans brought their numerical system to Britain.

One of the remaining mosaics has a star in the middle of it. The star was a symbol of good luck for the Romans.

Mosaics

Oh, I've run out of brown tiles.

The Romans used mosaics a lot for decoration or as a floor covering. It is the art of making pictures from thousands of little cubes of stone and a way of telling stories. Fourteen mosaics have been found at Isurium. The Romulus and Remus Mosaic (now in Leeds City Museum) tells the story of how Rome was founded by the twins in 753 BC – that's more than 1,000 years before Livia was born. Their dad was Mars, god of war, but the other gods were jealous and wanted to harm them so they were set afloat on a river to escape. They were later found and fed by a wolf and then brought up by a shepherd. Romulus and Remus wanted to be kings, so they built a city that was to become Rome. However, Romulus argued with Remus over who should be king and killed him.

...ABOUT AD 400 ROMANS LEAVE ISURIUM NEAR END OF ROMAN EMPIRE...

5

Here is an imaginary letter from Livia to her cousin, Chloe, back in Rome...

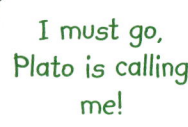

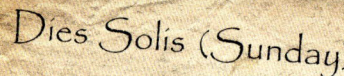

Dies Solis (Sunday)

Salve Chloe!
We have been here a month now: all the slaves have been hired and I have started lessons with my tutor, Plato. Geography is quite interesting (I can see that we are on the very edge of the Empire) and the history lesson about Julius Caesar's invasion of Britannia 250 years ago was good. I start learning Greek next week.

Yesterday we went by chariot along Dered Street to Eboracum. It was very busy, noisy and smelly in the main streets, the Via Principia and the Via Praetoria. The walls and the tower are massive! There's a huge bathhouse and an amphitheatre. There were a lot of ships on the river coming to and from the granaries.

It's better than I expected here. Father is busy and Mother enjoys running the villa. I must go now as Plato is calling.

Vale carissima Chloe! Livia
(Bye dearest Chloe! Livia)

Roman girls were often married at the age of 14. The marriages were arranged between the two families.

Livia! It's time for your studies. I shall be testing you on your Latin.

6

TUDOR
1485-1603

STUART
1603-1714

GEORGIAN
1714-1837

VICTORIAN
1837-1901

MODERN
TIMES
1902-NOW

D M FELICVLE
COIVGI KARIS
G M P F CVR

A tombstone of a woman was found at Aldborough. Her name was Felicula and her husband, Gaius, made the tribute. It roughly translates as: To...the departed Felicula, the most-caring wife. Her loyal and faithful husband Gaius saw to this.

This beautiful mosaic still survives and can be seen at Aldborough. The star was a symbol of good luck.

The Romans were ordered to leave Britain in AD 410 to try to save Rome from invaders.

How do we know?

At Aldborough you can still see parts of the town's defensive walls: they are 2·5 metres thick and 4 metres high. The walls and towers around Isurium were built in AD 200. Two of the four gates have also been excavated. The museum has lots of pottery on display which shows us how the Romans stored their food. The jewellery tells us that some of the Romans were quite rich; Livia's parents would have been wealthy as her father, Gaius, was a lawyer. The mosaics too tell us that some of the villas were very big and expensive. The Lion Mosaic was discovered by an inn keeper in 1832 when he was digging a grave to bury a dead calf. The Lion Mosaic would have reminded the owner of his hunting days in another part of the Empire where lions and wild boar were common.

The Viking Settlement

Magnus thinks back to his old life, before he arrived in England from Norway in AD 926. He had sailed up the Humber and then the River Ouse to Jorvik (the Viking name for York), in a long boat and then over land to the settlement just outside Harrogate. He is a skilled metalworker, learning from his travels in France and Germany, but there is plenty of work here for him. He lives in a street called Coppergate, which means street of the cup and bowl makers. There is demand for rings and necklaces, brooches and pins, as well as the metal bits of ice skates – and weapons in time of war.

Between the 8th and 11th centuries the Vikings took over most of northern Europe.

Sigmund's Hoard

Sigmund was chief of Magnus's settlement. He was very rich, mainly because of his trading and the booty he had won in many battles. He made his wealth in coins, jewellery, silver bowls and golden cups. Some of these had come from as far away as North Africa, Afghanistan and Uzbekistan. At this time the Anglo-Saxon King Athelstan was fighting the Vikings and taking back their lands. Sigmund was worried because Athelstan's armies were getting close. He decided to hide his riches in a gold-lined silver box, put it in a lead case and bury it in a secret place.

Viking place names
by = village
dale = valley
kirk = church
brig = bridge
garth = yard
force or foss = river

Viking Words

Many Viking words are still used today without us knowing! The Viking word for a street is gate. Harrogate comes from 'Harlo - gate', the road or way to Harlow (a large hill). Other words, or bits of words, which the Vikings brought to Britain are shown above. Can you think of any names or places today which are made from these Viking words? (eg Whitby).

Viking Coins

Coins were used for lots of different things apart from money. They were often made from silver and the heavier the coin the more valuable it was. Often coins were melted down to make jewellery. They also tell us a lot about the people who used them and their way of life. Coins can tell us who was in power and who the gods were. Athelstan captured Magnus's settlement in AD 927. Some of Sigmund's coins show that the Vikings were, at that time, mixing their traditional religion with Christianity – they have Thor, Viking god of war, on one side with St Peter on the other.

The Harrogate Hoard is one of the most important Viking discoveries in Britain for 150 years.

A Viking hoard was found at Goldsborough near Knaresborough in 1859. It contained brooches, arm rings and other jewellery. Many of the 39 coins were dhirams – Islamic coins from the Middle East.

SPOT THIS!

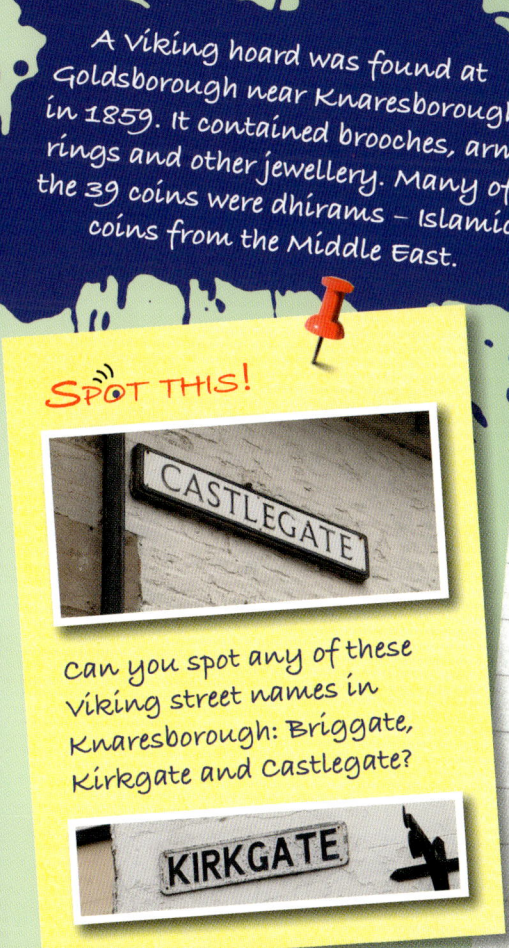

CASTLEGATE

Can you spot any of these Viking street names in Knaresborough: Briggate, Kirkgate and Castlegate?

KIRKGATE

How do we know?

One cold January day in 2007, David and Andrew Whelan went out for a day's metal detecting just outside Harrogate. They did not expect to discover a hoard of Viking treasure about 30 cm under the soil. It contained 617 coins and 65 other objects: jewellery, five arm bands, ingots and a gold and silver box – all valued later at over £1 million. This confirmed that a large Viking settlement existed near Harrogate around AD 900 and that its chief was very rich. Some of the items and coins came from as far away as modern-day Russia, North Africa, Uzbekistan and Afghanistan: proof that the Vikings travelled far and wide, trading as well as fighting. The hoard is being displayed in museums in Harrogate and York and in the British Museum.

Living in a Castle

There is much unrest in Knaresborough Castle. It is a cold day. The wind is whistling and the dogs are barking. The knight, Hugh de Morville, lives here with his family, but he is away at the moment, as he often is, helping King Henry II run the country. The servants huddle together and gossip saying "Canterbury is dead." These are troubled times, with the King forever falling out with the Archbishop of Canterbury. Who knows what will happen?

It is a sign of warning when Fluffy and Tinkles howl to the East.

In times of danger people took refuge at the castle.

Knaresborough Castle

Knaresborough castle was built by a Norman baron, Eustace Fitzjohn, in 1100. He had come over from Normandy with William the Conqueror in 1066. The castle is on top of a high cliff above the River Nidd. This location enabled the baron to guard and control the valley below. In 1170, Hugh de Morville lived at the castle. He was one of the four knights who murdered Thomas Becket in Canterbury Cathedral. Henry II told them to flee to Scotland but they took refuge in the castle for a year. They were very unpopular in Knaresborough because of their crime – even the dogs hated them.

Thomas Becket

Henry II made Thomas Archbishop of Canterbury in 1162. Although they were friends, they soon began arguing over issues such as whether bishops should be above the law. By 1170, Henry had had enough of Becket challenging his power and flew into a rage. He shouted, "What sluggards, what cowards have I brought up in my court, who care nothing for their allegiance to their lord. Who will rid me of this meddlesome priest?" Four of Henry's knights, including Hugh de Morville, heard this and took it as an order to kill Thomas. They rode to the Cathedral in Canterbury and hacked Thomas to death on the altar steps, just after Christmas 1170.

The East Gate of the castle

The Queen owns Knaresborough Castle; she will need to have a lot of work done if she ever wants to stay here instead of Windsor Castle!

I shall hide out in the castle. We shall be safe in there.

King John

In 1210, King John spent £1,290 (that was a lot of money then!) on the castle, making it one of his main strongholds in the north of England and a defence against raiding Scots and revolting barons. He made the moat bigger and you can still see the ditch where it was. King John often stayed at the castle when he came up to hunt in the Forest of Knaresborough.

On one of his visits to Knaresborough he gave gifts such as food and clothes to the poor for the first time in the castle. This was part of the religious Maundy service, a ceremony which dates back to around AD 600 where the king or queen give money to the poor on Maundy Thursday (the day before Good Friday). In 2010 the 800th anniversary of the first giving of Maundy Money in Knaresborough was celebrated.

Bless you my King.

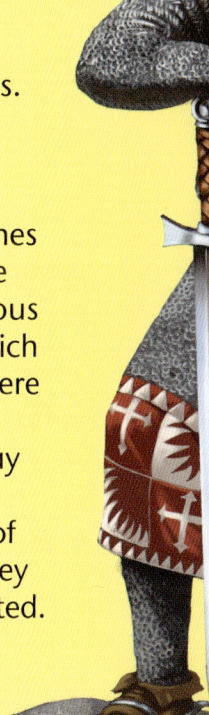

Here is an imaginary letter from Robert de Morville, Sir Hugh's son, to his friend Edward Slingsby in Ripon.

I love hunting in the forest. But you have to be careful, there are many beasts in there!

My dear Edward

Yesterday was a terrible day. Father had been away over Christmas and returned home with three of his fellow knights very agitated and unhappy. I think he had been to see the king in France and then sailed back to visit the archbishop in Canterbury – why he couldn't have just gone to York to see the archbishop there I'll never know! The servants are all gossiping, saying silly things like Canterbury is dead, but I don't believe them. The dogs keep barking and snarling for some strange reason. After dinner we took some horses from the stables and went hunting in the forest. The townsfolk seemed to be shunning us. Anyway, we killed two wild boar and a stag with our arrows. Unfortunately one of the men fell from his horse and broke his arm – he was screaming in agony. When we got back to the castle the cook gave him some brandy to shut him up. I must go now as father is calling.

Adieu

Robert

Knaresborough Castle has always been owned by Royalty. Many kings and queens have stayed here.

SPOT THIS!

Can you spot this mosaic outside of Knaresborough Castle. See how much history has happened in the castle!

TUDOR
1485-1603

STUART
1603-1714

GEORGIAN
1714-1837

VICTORIAN
1837-1901

MODERN
TIMES
1902-
NOW

Secret Tunnels

Sally ports were underground secret tunnels used in times of trouble. Only a few people such as the king knew about them. You can take a visit to Knaresborough Castle to see the tunnels which are 24 metres underground. These would have come in handy for the knights who didn't want to be seen.

This picture is from the Luttrell Psalter, showing the gruesome death of Thomas Becket.

Dear God, I pray for Becket to rest in peace. The poor chap got quite a bashing.

How do we know?

A monk, Edward Grim, who also wrote the story of Thomas Becket's life, watched the murder from a hiding place near the altar and was injured trying to help him. This is what he saw: "As to the fifth [knight]...he put his foot on the neck of the holy priest and precious martyr...calling out to the others, 'Let us away, knights; he will rise no more.'

There is a picture of Becket's death in the Luttrell Psalter, held in the British Library. It is one of the most famous English manuscripts of the Middle Ages: it contains beautiful pictures of everyday life, especially of the rich, in the 14th century.

    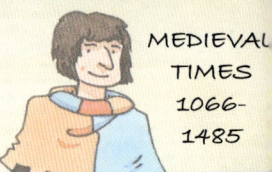

Mother Shipton

The worried husband and wife hurry across the muddy path to the small house. They have travelled far after hearing of Mother Shipton's prophecies. Some people say she is a witch and the Devil's daughter, but the couple have nothing to lose. Their daughter is sick and they seek Mother Shipton's wise words. Perhaps she can save their daughter. After all, Mother Shipton has the power to foretell the future.

St John's Well still stands today although it is no longer used.

Harrogate Spa

The first spring in Harrogate was discovered by William Slingsby in 1571. After drinking from a well, Slingsby said the water tasted the same as the spring water from the town of Spa, now in Belgium, where people believed the water had healing properties. He called the well Tewit Well. The Sweet Spa (St John's Well) was later discovered in 1631. These wells made Harrogate grow into one of the most famous spas in Europe with its 88 different springs. Many inns were built to accommodate the surge of visitors who wanted to take the waters which contain minerals. Among the conditions thought to be curable by the waters were indigestion, flatulence, 'hysterical affections' and chronic alcoholism.

The Prophetess

Mother Shipton was born in 1488 in a cave on the banks of the River Nidd in Knaresborough. She was a famous prophetess – that means she could tell what was going to happen in the future. Her visions became known throughout the country. Some people said she was a witch and the Devil's daughter. She knew about the Great Fire of London before it happened in 1666 and she foretold the date of her own death in 1567. For all we know she may even have known that Knaresborough castle would be destroyed by Oliver Cromwell, that King James II would have a school named after him in Knaresborough and that Harrogate would become a famous spa...

SPOT THIS!

The Petrifying Well is one of the oldest visitor attractions in Knaresborough. The waters high mineral content means it turns everything in its path to stone. See if your teddy turns to stone!

John Ray visited the spa at Harrogate in 1661 and described the waters as follows: "stinks noisomely of rotten eggs or sulphur".

Why do we have to speak Latin all the time. It's so hard!

King James's School, Knaresborough

King James's School opened as an all-boys school in 1616. In the early days it was very strict. Anyone "unapte to learn" was expelled, as was anyone who was absent, unless they were ill. The teachers were allowed to cane you for "swearing, lying, picking, stealing, fighting... wanton speech and unclean behaviour". School started at 6.00 am in the summer, 7.00 am in winter. In assembly every morning you had to get on your knees and say the longest Psalm there is (Psalm 119 with 167 verses), the Creed and the Lord's Prayer. After Year 1 you had to speak in Latin at all times, including playtime, and your mum and dad had to supply books and pens, candles in winter and bows and arrows (so that you could practise in case there was a war). The school became a mixed school in 1971 and is still there today; some of you may even go there.

CELT
500 BC

ROMAN
AD 43-410

ANGLO-SAXON
AD 450-1066

VIKING
AD 865-1066

MEDIEVAL
TIMES
1066-1485

Civil War

The King, Charles I, was fighting Oliver Cromwell to decide who ruled England. Knaresborough was on the King's side. After the Battle of Marston Moor (in between Knaresborough and York) in 1644, Oliver Cromwell laid siege to Knaresborough Castle when some of the King's men took refuge there. He starved them out and destroyed most of the castle leaving it in the condition you see today. Sir Henry Slingsby, the local MP and member of a secret society called the Sealed Knot, was executed on Tower Hill in London in 1658 because he kept trying to bring the monarchy back after Oliver Cromwell had executed Charles I. Sir Henry's body, minus his head, was returned to Knaresborough where it still lies in the Slingsby Chapel in St John's Church. The bloodstained shirt he wore when his head was chopped off is preserved.

A legend has grown up around the attempt by Mrs Whincup to save the life of a young Knaresborough boy during the siege; this could be her message…

My Lord Colonel Lilburne

I beg you to spare the life of John Plowman. He was only doing what any dutiful son would do for his father - trying to save his life. The wretched people in the castle have had no fresh water or food now for nearly three weeks; they are very weak. John was simply trying to get food to them, rowing across the moat and braving the fire of Cromwell's men and the cannonballs of your soldiers. Hanging him will deter no one. Why not spare him and celebrate his courage instead? Your mercy will be rewarded in Heaven.

Charles I was tried, convicted and executed for treason.

I seem to have lost my head.

This painting shows the Battle of Marston Moor. After the Royalists (King's men) were defeated, they lost control over northern England.

SPOT THIS!

Have you seen the King's Tower? It was the height of fashion when it was built in the early 14th century.

> Knaresborough has witnessed some important times in history.

How do we know?

During the Civil War a series of battles was fought between the Royalists (supporters of King Charles I) and the Roundheads (supporters of Parliament). Marston Moor was the bloodiest battle of the Civil War. Although the King's men were defeated, Knaresborough Castle remained a supporter of King Charles. An Act of Parliament in 1646 ordered the demolition of many Royalist castles, including Knaresborough. In 1648 demolition began. Nearly all the buildings within the castle walls were destroyed, except for the Courthouse and the King's Tower. The town's people had petitioned and managed to save the King's Tower which remained standing and continued to be used as a prison.

Rich and Poor

A couple dressed in their finery walk arm-in-arm towards the imposing building. They have promised a generous donation to Bath Hospital. The medical officer and matron are going to show them round. In his letter of invitation the medical officer explained that the hospital has 25 beds for the sick people who live at least 5 km away. The patients will benefit from taking the waters thanks to the donations of the couple and others from society.

People worried that disease would spread where sick people took the waters. This led to four well heads being built in 1772.

Bath Hospital

80% of the population of England had worms at the time.

Spa towns often attracted rich people who wanted to be seen to be part of 'good society'. They were part of what was called 'the gentry.' A part of the social scene was philanthropy – where the richer people looked after the poorer people in some way. At this time it was very difficult for poor people to get medical care when they needed it and often they just had to put up with their illnesses. The Bath Hospital (later renamed the Royal Bath Hospital) was built in 1824 to help the less well off: it depended entirely on donations from the rich. The hospital only ever had 45 beds at its peak. It was rebuilt in Victorian times and the low, plain building was replaced with a grander more luxurious building. The hospital and treatment continued to be paid for by donations until the hospital closed in 1994.

...1717 BLIND JACK BORN...

Blind Jack

Blind Jack is a local legend around Harrogate and Knaresborough. His real name was John Metcalfe and he was a true Jack of All Trades despite the fact that he was blind. Before he found his true skill as a road builder, Jack was a musician in the army (playing at the Battle of Culloden), a hunter, a horse dealer, a smuggler and a cock-fight gambler. Amazingly for a blind man he built over 290 km of roads in the north of England.

SPOT THIS!

Can you find the statue of Blind Jack, with his viameter? He used his viameter to measure distances.

Blind Jack is still around Knaresborough today. A pub has been named after him, his name is on a road and he has a plaque in his memory.

BLIND JACK'S

The Stray

Strays are large areas of common land in towns and cities where freemen were allowed to graze their cattle. In 1770, in Harrogate, 80 hectares of grassy land were made into strays so that people could get to the springs and take exercise – exercise was just as important as the waters as people recognized it helped them stay healthy. For Queen Victoria's Jubilee in 1887 a huge barbecue was held on the Stray. The townsfolk roasted an ox for 24 hours, ate 4,000 buns and drank 2,200 litres of beer. In World War Two they dug trenches to stop enemy planes landing there. Every year a big funfair is held on the Stray.

Harrogate. The Stray II.

The Stray remains a public area and is popular for picnics and ball games, but how has it changed from this old photograph?

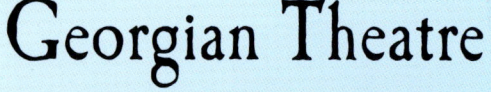

Georgian Theatre

Entertainment was an important activity in any fashionable town like Harrogate. The Georgian Theatre was built in 1788 by Thomas Wilks (who ran the Granby Hotel) next door to stage the theatre productions he held in his barn. The theatre closed in 1830 and is now a private house called Mansfield House. The Town Hall Theatre opened in 1882. The famous d'Oyley Carte Company and Lily Langtry performed there. The Opera House opened in 1900 and became famous for its pantomimes. Entertainment continued to be in demand and the Kursaal opened in 1903. Now called the Royal Hall it has recently been beautifully restored.

This is an imaginary diary extract of a young girl called Helen who has been to the theatre with her parents.

This evening after dinner we all went to the theatre in Church Square to see a farce called "The Humours of Harrogate" written by Francis Meek. Everyone laughed their heads off — it wasn't that funny though.

The place was packed and everyone was dressed up in their best clothes, especially the people in the boxes. (We were in the pit, but at least that's better than the gallery!) The scenery was beautifully painted — as were the actors' faces! What with the balls and assemblies Harrogate has become quite the place and caters well for the social lives of we who come to take the waters!

I had better...

> The theatre, the theatre. How I do love the theatre!

This poster tells us the performances showing at the Theatre Royal in 1810.

LAST NIGHT BUT TWO.

THEATRE ROYAL, HARROGATE.

On TUESDAY Evening the 18th of SEPTEMBER, 1810.
THEIR MAJESTIES' SERVANTS,
will perform a favourite TRAGEDY, (written by Shakespeare) called,

KING RICHARD III.

Containing some of the most remarkable events in the English History, as the Death of King Henry the sixth—The Murder of the two young Princes in the Tower—The Marriage of Richard and Lady Ann—Death of the Duke of Buckingham—The Landing of Henry the Seventh—and the downfall of the crook-back Tyrant, at the bloody battle of Bosworth Field, being the last that was fought between the House of York and Lancaster.

King Richard, by a THESPIAN, from YORK.
King Henry   Mr   WILSON
Duke of Buckingham   Mr   GEORGE
Prince Edward Master MEADOWS—Duke of York Master BUTLER
Tressel   Mr   BUTLER
Lord Stanley   Mr   MARTIN—Catesby Mr   G. BUTLER
Lord Mayor   Mr   DAVIS—Ratcliffe Mr   DUNNING
Lieutenant of the Tower Mr SMITHSON—Oxford Mr HALLAM
Earl of Richmond   by   A GENTLEMAN,
(His First Appearance on any Stage)
Lady Ann   Mrs   MURRAY
Dutchess of York   Mrs   MARTIN
The Queen   Mrs   BUTLER
To which will be added a Musical FARCE, called,

ROSINA:
OR LOVE IN A COTTAGE.

An old painting of people gathering around the Harrogate Spa Well in the 1770s

The rich and famous used to visit Harrogate's theatres when they came to take the waters. Today the theatre is affordable for everyone, not just the rich, and the Royal Hall continues to attract visitors.

88 springs were found altogether. People could bathe in the water from the Spa as well as drink it: 36 in Valley Gardens alone.

How do we know?

In 1623, Dr Edmund Deane wrote a book called *The English Spaw Fountaine* in which he described the Tewit Well and the healthy waters that came from it. Dr Deane tells us how even Queen Elizabeth I's doctor, Timothy Bright, recommended the waters. One of the things Harrogate Spa cured was worms, Deane said. It was partly due to Deane's book that Harrogate became so famous which led to the theatres opening.

Before the Georgian Theatre opened, according to Hollins's 1858 *Illustrated Handbook*, "theatrical representations were performed in a barn behind the Granby Hotel; and there it was that the celebrated Miss Melon used to delight her audience, and where her genius shone forth in a blaze of triumph, which completely obscured the light of twelve penny candles flickering in bottles around her."

The Royal Pump Room

It is very smelly inside the Royal Pump Room. Jane has taken her first tumbler of spa water for the day. Her parents hope that the waters will cure her ill health. Apparently Harrogate has the smelliest waters in the world because of the sulphur, so they must be good! Jane is glad to step outside and take in the fresh air. She and her maid stroll towards the bandstand, nodding their heads to other fine folk taking their exercise. The band is already playing. What a fine day this will be.

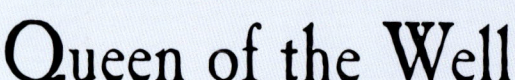

The Royal Baths became the leading centre in the world for hydrotherapy treatment.

Queen of the Well

Betty Lupton was a well-woman who served at the Royal Pump Room. She was called 'Queen of the Well' and was a familiar sight as she ladled out the waters to her customers. She retired in 1843. Some people say that Bettys Tea Rooms were named after her when they opened in 1919. Other baths in Harrogate included the Montpellier Baths and Gardens (opened 1834), Cheltenham Pump Room, the Victoria Baths (1834), the new Victoria Baths (opened 1871) and the Royal Baths (opened 1897).

Betty Lupton was a voluntary water server.

The Railways Are Coming

The railways came to Harrogate and Knaresborough in 1848. They brought more and more tourists and helped make Harrogate into a very popular spa town. At Knaresborough they had to build a viaduct, or railway bridge, to carry the railway lines over the River Nidd. It was 23 metres high and 86 metres long with four arches. Just before it was finished disaster struck when the bridge collapsed into the river. It took two more years to rebuild — and that's the bridge you can still see today. Before the railways came a stage coach. It would take about four days to get to London. The new trains took about 13 hours.

The viaduct still stands over the River Nidd.

Knaresborough Water Carnival

This magnificent spectacle was held every year. The firework company, Brock's, gave an awesome firework display after dark during which the viaduct was changed into Niagara Falls and a man called Pedro crossed the river on a tightrope. There was a fairy castle and an Eiffel Tower, and 40 dancers danced and a brass band played on the *Marigold*, a houseboat on the River Nidd.

SPOT THIS!

You can get a free drink from the water pump outside the Royal Pump Room Museum.

Visitors flocked to Knaresborough Water Carnival to see the amazing display the town put on.

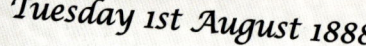
Here is an imaginary letter Jane Maurice has written to her friend, describing her daily routine while staying in Harrogate to take the waters.

> I am quite exhausted after my day!

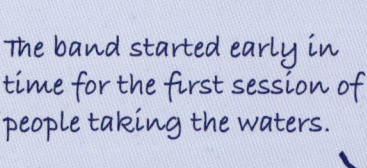

Tuesday 1st August 1888

Dear Charlotte

We are now quite settled here in Harrogate and are enjoying the social scene very much. It is recommended that one stays for three weeks if one is to get any long-term benefit. A trip to Scarborough is then encouraged. Here is my daily routine:

7.00 – 8.00 am	Rise and visit Pump Room for first tumbler of water
8.00 am	Walk about, listening to the band
8.15 am	Take second tumbler of water
8.15 – 9.00 am	Listen to the band and if prescribed take third tumbler of water
9.00 am	Breakfast. For some people it is advisable that they drive; either by omnibus, carriage or bath chair, but the walk home can be advantageous if it can be accomplished without undue fatigue. Care should be taken to avoid exertion.
10.00 – 11.00 am	Morning paper or letter writing
11.30 am	Second visit to Pump Room
1.00 pm	Rest for half an hour
1.30 pm	Lunch to be followed by one hour of rest.
3.30 pm	Afternoon driving, walking, cycling, golfing or third visit to the Pump Room.
4.30 pm	Afternoon tea in the gardens
7.00 pm	Dinner. Concert room
10.00 pm	Bed

Yours
Jane

The band started early in time for the first session of people taking the waters.

HARROGATE. VALLEY GARDENS. TEA PAVILION

The Royal Baths was Harrogate's grandest building and the world's most advanced hydrotherapy centre.

The Montpellier Baths building was demolished in 1896. Take a look at the clothes people are wearing. How have they changed?

A dead dog in a bath? Whatever next?

How do we know?

We know that people, including doctors, had reason to believe in the health-giving qualities of the waters in Harrogate because a man called Thorpe carried out a chemical analysis of the Pump Room waters in 1875. This is what he said:

"Proven to be beneficial in most forms of Indigestion; Constipation, Flatulence and Acidity. For all cases of functional disorders of the liver. For stimulating the action of the kidneys and in all forms of Chronic Skin Diseases. To be drunk warm or cold. Dosage between 10-24 ounces to be taken early in the morning."

In 1821 people complained about vandalism: "during the night some persons unknown...have put into the mineral springs some quantities of Dung, Ashes, Dead Dogs, and other animals of a most offensive nature."

In 1841 the Harrogate Improvement Act was passed to protect the springs.

Fairs of the North

The doors open and everyone rushes forward. Inside there are rows and rows of every toy you can imagine! Mum said we could bring our favourite toy to get it valued. I've got my doll that Granny gave me for my fifth birthday and my brother Tom has brought his collection of toy cars. We've been saving up our pocket money to buy some bargain toys!

Changing Town

Harrogate's popularity as a spa town began to decline in the 1930s. Medicine was getting better and people were able to find more effective cures for their ailments locally. And with the advances in travel, more people were taking holidays abroad.

During World War Two, many of London's government offices were moved and Harrogate's large hotels became their headquarters. With the spas closing down the Council had to find other ways to bring people into the town. It had the fine buildings from the old spas and it had land so it decided to make Harrogate into a centre for conferences, fairs and shows. One of the most famous is the Harrogate Toy Fair.

Another popular event is the Great Yorkshire Show, set up by the Yorkshire Agricultural Society in 1837. This show moved around Yorkshire before it became a permanent event in Harrogate in 1951.

Show jumping competitor at the Great Yorkshire Show 2010

...1960 THE TOY FAIR COMES TO HARROGATE...

TUDOR
1485-1603

STUART
1603-1714

GEORGIAN
1714-1837

VICTORIAN
1837-1901

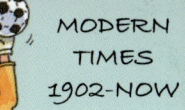
MODERN
TIMES
1902-NOW

The Oldest Chemist Shop

This shop in Knaresborough opened in 1720 and was a chemist's shop until 1965. You can still see a huge pestle and mortar used for grinding up all kinds of potions and medicines and rows of medicine bottles, including one for leeches. The old couch is there where the chemist used to bleed his patients and extract teeth.

Aargh!

The 1982 Eurovision song contest was held in Harrogate.

SPOT THIS!

Can you see the old medicine bottles lined up in the Oldest Chemist Shop?

Take a look inside the Oldest Chemist Shop and see what you can find.

Oh yay, oh yay! Come to Knaresborough today!

Knaresborough FEVA

Every summer since 1996, Knaresborough has held an entertainment and visual arts festival that goes on for ten days. The non-profit-making festival is run by people in the community and attracts many visitors. From plays in the park to art trails and exhibitions, Knaresborough continues to draw in tourists for its amazing history and culture.

CELT 500 BC	ROMAN AD 43-410	ANGLO-SAXON AD 450-1066	VIKING AD 865-1066	MEDIEVAL TIMES 1066-1485

Harrogate and Knaresborough Today and Tomorrow...

Harrogate and Knaresborough are popular tourist towns today with many people having happy memories of times spent here. What do you think visitors will remember when they come for holidays in twenty years' time? Will it be the same things or do you think there will be different attractions?

Harrogate's motto is 'Arx celebris fontibus', which means 'a citadel famous for its springs'.

Since 1919, Bettys Tea Rooms have served delicious cakes and teas at tables overlooking the Stray and Montpellier Gardens. Not many cafés can claim 90 years of business!

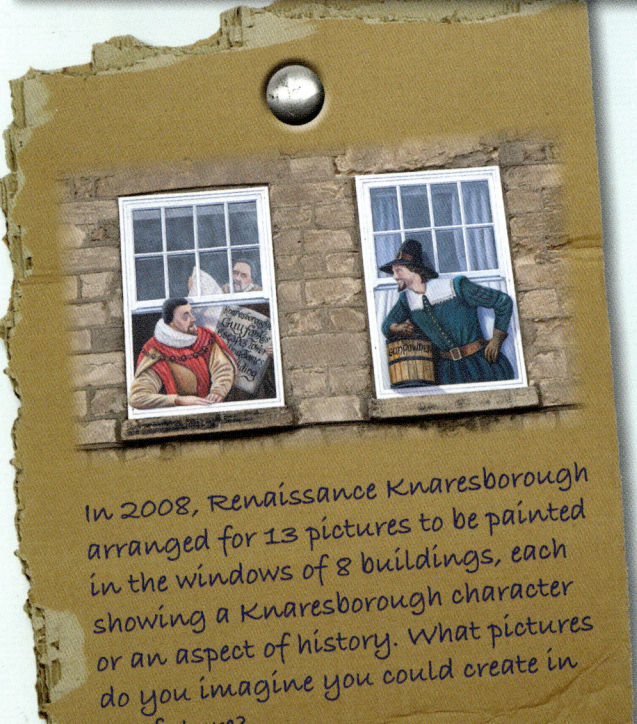

In 2008, Renaissance Knaresborough arranged for 13 pictures to be painted in the windows of 8 buildings, each showing a Knaresborough character or an aspect of history. What pictures do you imagine you could create in the future?

Menwith Hill is an RAF base near Harrogate which contains a missile warning site; it listens to radio messages from all around the world. It is the largest electronic monitoring station in the world. Who do you think we might be listening to in the next 20 years?

The Great Yorkshire Show in Harrogate has hundreds of competitions and stalls with prizes for the best cows, sheepdogs, horses and other animals. How do you think this will change, if at all, in the future?

I fancy one of Bett's fat rascals. Yum!

SPOT THIS!

The Great Knaresborough Bed Race has become famous for its colourful and eccentric teams. Held every year for the last 45 years, teams gather at Knaresborough Castle and race through the medieval streets.

The Knaresborough Bookshop has been selling books in the town for over 40 years. With electronic books and books downloadable from the internet how do you think people will read books in the future?

Harrogate International Centre is one of the biggest conference centres in the UK, holding many different conferences and exhibitions. What sort of exhibitions do you imagine it might be holding in 2050?

How will they know?

Look around you. Which buildings do you think will be standing 200 years from now? What records do we keep that other people might one day read? Do DVDs and computers change what we can leave behind? What would you put in a time capsule? What will remain for historians in the future to find out about 21st-century Harrogate and Knaresborough?

Glossary

AD – a short way of writing the Latin words anno Domini, which mean 'in the year of our Lord', i.e. after the birth of Christ.

Amphitheatre – a round, open-air theatre, surrounded by seats which rise from the centre so everyone can see.

Amphorae – Roman two-handled narrow-necked jars.

Artefact – an object, often an archaeological one.

Bath chair – an early form of wheelchair with three wheels.

BC – a short way of writing 'before the birth of Christ'.

Cavalrymen – soldiers who fight on horseback.

Excavate – to dig into the earth to find things buried there, so we can learn about the past.

Exhibition – a public display of products.

Fortress – a large, strong building or fort offering support and protection.

Gentry – people of high social class.

Hoard – a store of food or money, hidden for future use.

Isurium Brigantum – the Roman name for the town of Aldborough.

Luttrell Psalter – an illuminated manuscript written and illustrated around 1325–1335.

Martyr – a person who suffers or dies for a cause or belief.

Maundy Money – special money given by the king or queen to the poor on the day before Good Friday.

Middle Ages – a period of time roughly from AD 1000 to the 15th century.

Moat – a wide ditch, filled with water, that surrounds a castle.

Mosaics – designs or decorations made up of small pieces of coloured glass or stone.

Omnibus – a horse-drawn bus.

Pestle and mortar – a tool used to crush, grind and mix things. The pestle is a bat-shaped stick and the mortar is a bowl.

Prophecy – a prediction about the future.

Pump Room – a room at a spa where spring water is pumped for people to drink.

Roundhead – anyone who fought on the side of Parliament against Charles I in the English Civil War.

Royalist – anyone who fought on the side of King Charles I in the English Civil War.

Sally ports – secret underground tunnels.

Sealed Knot Society – a secret committee of Royalists who tried to help Charles I during the English Civil War.

Siege – when people try to capture a place by surrounding or blockading it.

Spa – a mineral spring where the waters are believed to be good for the health.

Strays – large areas of common land in cities where freemen were allowed to graze their cattle.

Theatre – a building where plays and operas are performed.

Viaduct – a bridge for carrying a road or railway across a valley.

Viameter – a measuring wheel used to measure distance.

Index

Aldborough, 4, 5, 7
Aldborough Museum, 5, 7
Athelstan, 8, 9

Bath Hospital, 18
Becket, Thomas (Archbishop of
    Canterbury), 10, 11, 12, 13
Bettys Tea Rooms, 22, 28
Brigantes tribe, 4, 5
Briggate Street, 9

Castlegate Street, 9
Charles I, 16, 17
Cheltenham Pump Room, 22
Church Square, 20
Coppergate Street, 8
Cromwell, Oliver, 16

Deane, Dr Edmund, 21

Elizabeth I, 21
English Civil War, 15, 16, 17
Eurovision Song Contest, 27

Fitzjohn, Eustace, 10

Georgian Theatre (Mansfield
    House), 20, 21
Goldsborough, 9
Granby Hotel, 20, 21
Great Knaresborough Bed Race
    29
Great Yorkshire Show, 26, 29
Grim, Edward, 13

Harrogate Hoard, 9
Harrogate Improvement Act, 25
Harrogate International Centre,
    29
Harrogate Spa, 14
Harrogate Toy Fair, 26
Henry II, 10, 11

Isurium Brigantum, 4, 5, 7

Jack, Blind (John Metcalfe), 19
John, 11

King James's School, 15
King's Tower, 17
Kirkgate Street, 9
Knaresborough Bookshop, 29
Knaresborough Castle, 10, 11,
    12, 13, 16, 17
Knaresborough FEVA, 27
Knaresborough, Forest of, 11
Knaresborough Water Carnival,
    23
Kursaal (Royal Hall), 20, 21

Lion Mosaic, 7
Lupton, Betty (Queen of the
    Well), 22
Luttrell Psalter, 13

Mansfield House (Georgian
    Theatre), 20, 21
Marston Moor, Battle of, 16, 17
Maundy Money, 11
Menwith Hill, 28
Metcalfe, John (Blind Jack), 19
Montpellier Baths and Gardens,
    22, 25, 28
Morville, Hugh de, 10, 11

Oldest Chemist Shop, 27
Opera House, 20

Petrifying Well, 15

Queen Victoria's Jubilee, 19

Renaissance Knaresborough,
    28
River Nidd, 10, 23

Romulus and Remus Mosaic, 5
Royal Baths, 22, 25
Royal Hall (Kursaal), 20, 21
Royal Pump Room, 22, 24, 25
Royal Pump Room Museum, 23

St John's Church, 16
St John's Well, 14
Sally ports, 13
Sealed Knot Society, 16
Shipton, Mother, 14, 15
Slingsby, Sir Henry, 16
Slingsby, William, 14
Stray, the, 19, 28

Tewit Well, 14, 21
Town Hall Theatre, 20

Valley Gardens, 21
viaduct, 23
Victoria Baths, 22

Whelan, David and Andrew, 9
Whincup, Mrs, 16
William the Conqueror, 10
World War Two, 19, 26

Acknowledgements

The author and publishers would like to thank the following people for their generous help:
Gavin Holman for his generosity and help, www.satiche.org.uk;
Conrad Plowman for the use of the Knaresborough Carnival image
and Laura Crisp and all at Bettys Tea Rooms

The publishers would like to thank the following people and organizations
for their permission to reproduce material on the following pages:
p5: Fishbourne Museum, Portsmouth; p7: English Heritage Photo Library; p9: The Trustees of the British Museum;
p13: The British Library Board. (Add.42130,f.51); p15: The Daniel Heighton Travel Photography Collection/Alamy;
p17: Battle of Marston Moor, 1644 by Barker, John (19th century) © Cheltenham Art Gallery & Museums, Gloucestershire,
UK/The Bridgeman Art Library; p19: Gavin Holman; p20: Copyright North Yorkshire County Council Unnetie Digital
Archive; p21: Gavin Holman; p22: Gavin Holman; p23: Conrad Plowman; p24: Gavin Holman; p25: Copyright North
Yorkshire County Council Unnetie Digital Archive; p26: Image kindly provided by the Yorkshire Agricultural Society;
p28: Bettys Tea Rooms; Paul Thompson Images/Alamy, A Renaissance Knaresborough Project;
p29: Image kindly provided by the Yorkshire Agricultural Society, Nigel Perry

All other images copyright of Hometown World

Written by Paul Chrystal and Anne Chrystal
Educational consultant: Neil Thompson
Local history consultant: Malcolm Neesam
Designed by Stephen Prosser

Illustrated by Leo Brown, Kate Davies, Dynamo Ltd, Mike Hall, Peter Kent, John MacGregor,
Leighton Noyes and Tim Sutcliffe
Additional photographs by Alex Long

First published by HOMETOWN WORLD in 2010
Hometown World Ltd
7 Northumberland Buildings
Bath BA1 2JB

www.hometownworld.co.uk